DEEP COUNTRY VIBES

A Journey Through Life, Love, and Country
Music with Trace Adkins

By

William J. Stewart

TABLE OF CONTENT

INTRODUCTION

Country music artist and actor Trace Adkins was born in 1962. His record-breaking debut album, "Dreamin' Out Loud,' ' which included singles like "Every Light in the House,' ' marked the beginning of his career in the late 1990s. Traditional country music and Adkins's deep voice made him popular very fast.

He carried on putting out popular albums over the years, such as "Big Time" and "Chrome." With hits like "Ladies Love Country Boys" and "You're Gonna Miss This," Adkins' career rose to unprecedented heights. He pursued acting and made appearances in TV series and movies in addition to his musical accomplishments.

Adkins persisted in spite of obstacles in his personal life, such as a 2011 fire that destroyed his home. Being a renowned person with an interesting path, his talent and tenacity have cemented his place in the country music world.

Staying loyal to his country origins, Trace Adkins experimented with other musical styles in the years that followed, continuing to grow as an artist. Recordings such as "Songs About Me" and "Dangerous Man" demonstrated his adaptability and capacity to engage a wide range of listeners.

Even though Adkins struggled with alcoholism and other personal issues, he faced them head-on, got support, and overcame them in the end. Many followers found him accessible because of his candor about his experiences, which gave his persona more dimension.

Adkins stayed active in the entertainment business outside of music, taking part in reality series like "Celebrity Apprentice" and even coming in second in 2008. Beyond the music industry, his popularity grew as a result of his captivating personality, which won over a wider following.

Adkins released a number of popular albums throughout the years, including "Love Will..." and "Something's Going On." He received several honors and accolades for his contributions to country music, which cemented his reputation in the industry.

The path of Trace Adkins is a monument to tenacity, fortitude, and the tremendous ability of music to elicit strong human emotions. He's still a major player in the country music scene, whether it's because of his emotional songs or his on-screen persona.

Trace Adkins has demonstrated his steadfast skill and dedication to his trade often in recent years. The albums "Something's Going On" and "Ain't That Kind of Cowboy," which came out later, showed that he was still open to experimenting with various musical genres and ideas, which kept his work current and interesting.

Because of his strong stage presence and rich, rich voice, Adkins' live performances continue to be the highlights of his career. Fans may now witness the unadulterated passion and genuineness that characterize his music as he travels the nation on his tours.

Adkins has been a committed philanthropist who has supported a range of charity initiatives in addition to his musical endeavors. Adding even more significance to his legacy, his participation in programs such as the Wounded Warrior Project symbolizes his commitment to helping those in need.

Having worked in the country music industry for many years, Trace Adkins is a seasoned performer who has made a lasting impression. In addition to being a beloved character in country music, he has also gained popularity due to his ability to relate to listeners via his music and his candor about facing difficulties in life. His path will always have resonance.

CHAPTER ONE

The Biography of Trace Adkins

American country music singer and actor Tracy
Darrell Adkins was born on January 13, 1962.
Dreamin' Out Loud, Adkins' debut album on
Capitol Records Nashville, was released in 1996.
He has since put out two Greatest Hits
collections and eleven additional studio albums.
Adkins has also had over 20 singles chart on
Billboard's country music charts. Three of his
successes, "(This Ain't) No Thinkin' Thing,"
"Ladies Love Country Boys," and "You're
Gonna Miss This," were number-one hits and
reached their peaks in 1997, 2007, and 2008,
respectively. On the Canadian country charts, "I
Left Something Turned on at Home" peaked at
number one. In the US, his studio albums have
received at least six gold or platinum
certifications. Songs About Me from 2005 is his
best-selling album to date; it has sold two

million copies and has been certified two times platinum. Adkins is renowned for having a unique bass-baritone speaking and singing voice. In addition, he has made numerous television appearances, such as voicing lead character Alby Roman on Monarch, a panelist on the game shows Hollywood Squares and Pyramids, an All-Star Celebrity Apprentice finalist in 2008 and winner in 2013, a recurring character on King of the Hill named Elvin, and narrating television commercials for KFC and Firestone. In late 2007, Adkins also published his autobiography, A Personal Stand: Observations and Opinions from a Free-Thinking Roughneck. Among the movies in which he has acted are Mom's Night Out, The Lincoln Lawyer, and I Can Only Imagine.

Early Childhood And Education

The son of Aaron Doyle Adkins and Peggy Callaway, Adkins was born in Sarepta, Louisiana. James W. Callaway (1923–2008), a Christian musician, was his maternal uncle. At the juvenile age of 10, Adkins developed an interest in music; his father purchased a guitar for him and engaged a teacher. Adkins joined a gospel group named The New Commitments while attending the now-closed Sarepta High School. He belonged to the FFA as well. Adkins subsequently studied at Ruston at Louisiana Tech University. Adkins was a walk-on offensive tackle for the Louisiana Tech Bulldogs football team. A knee injury sustained during his freshman season prevented him from playing for the team. Adkins was never a graduate. He was employed on an oil rig following his college graduation. In addition, he was a member of the Bayeux band. Adkins was a pharmacy technician as well before deciding to become a musician. After cutting his left pinky finger off in an accident while trying to open a pail with a knife, he requested that the surgeons replace it at an angle so he could keep playing the guitar. Before relocating to Nashville, Tennessee in 1992, Adkins played at honky-tonk bars around the Ark-La-Tex region for the following several years. Adkins got to know Nashville-based

Arista Records executive Rhonda Follow at the end of 1994. Over the following two years, Adkins was heard by many of Follow's friends in the music business. One night, while Adkins was playing at Tilly and Lucy's pub in Mount Juliet, Tennessee, Scott Hendricks of the Nashville Capitol "on the spot" signed him to a deal.

Between 2001 and 2004

Adkins had to briefly postpone the tour in 2001 due to injuries sustained in a tractor accident. He went to his 28-day inpatient alcohol treatment facility in Nashville not long after the Chrome record was released. On the country album chart, Chrome became the first album to reach the top five. At the close of 2002, the lead single made it into the top 10. The Greatest Hits Collection and Comin' On Strong were Adkins' two 2003 albums. He received his Grand Ole Opry Hall of Fame induction the same year. In addition, he voiced Center Square in a KFC commercial and made an appearance on the game show Hollywood Squares. Of this compilation of best hits, only the song 'Then They Do' was published. Two singles were released from the album, which carried over the Greatest Hits Collection: "Hot Mama," which reached number five, and "Rough and Ready," which peaked at number thirteen. In the television episode of Yes, Dear (Greg & Jimmy's Criminals) that aired in February 2004, Adkins and Travis Tritt portrayed prisoners.

Between 2005 and 2007

Adkins' album Songs About Me was published in March 2005. In December 2004, the first single, "Title," was made available. The topic of "Arlington," the second single off the album, which was written in the first person by a fictitious soldier who was about to be buried in Arlington National Cemetery, caused controversy. After that, "Honky Tonk Badonkadonk" became a crossover smash and was Adkins's first Top 40 appearance on the Billboard Hot 100. Dangerous Man, Adkins' seventh studio album, was made available in

2006. Swing, the initial song from the album, peaked at number twenty. "Ladies Love Country Boys," the album's second number-one hit on the country chart, becoming Adkins' first since "(This Ain't) No Thinkin' Thing" in 1997. The music video for "Ladies Love Country Boys" features Briana, Adkins' daughter. The last single off the album, "I Wanna Feel Something," did not do well in the charts. Consequently, Adkins declared he would no longer be supporting the song. "I Got My Game On" is a single that Adkins released in August 2007. The song's working title was "Game On," and it was originally intended to be the opening track of a new album. But instead of releasing a full-length album, Adkins chose to release American Man: Greatest Hits Volume II, a second greatest hits collection featuring "I Got My Game On" as the lead single. Adkins' fastest-rising second single to date, "You're Gonna Miss This," was also released off the album. Additionally, "You're Gonna Miss This" earned her third consecutive number-one hit for a hot country song and her most successful single ever on the Hot Digital

Songs (#8), Billboard Hot 100 (#12), and Billboard Pop 100 (#19) charts. A Personal Stand: Observations and Opinions from a Free-Thinking Roughneck was the title of Adkins' debut book when it was released.

Between 2008 and 2009

The lead single from X, "Muddy Water," was released by Adkins on November 25th, 2008. In the "Muddy Water" music video, Stephen Baldwin, a competitor on Celebrity Apprentice, plays a man who was baptized in a murky river and subsequently contacted Adkins as a friend. The song peaked at number 22 on the country charts after entering the top 30. Released as the album's second and third singles, "Marry for Money" and "All I Ask for Anymore" both peaked at number 14 on the country charts. The Macy's Thanksgiving Day Parade included Adkins in November 2008. On the "Jimmy Dean" float, he sang the hit song "You're Gonna Miss This" with his family. A local Kansas City ad promoting season tickets and the 50th season of the National Football League's Kansas City Chiefs featured Adkins in 2009. Adkins sang a duet for law enforcement and firemen in the US and Canada called "My First Ride," co-written by country music icon Ronnie Milsap. Furthermore, the label politely declined to allow radio stations to play the song once it was released. Leading a demonstration against Capitol Records, Milsap demanded "Free Trace" and the playback of the song. Starting in November 2009, Adkins went on the Shine All-Night Tour, sharing the main stage alongside Martina McBride as a country artist. He also recorded a duet with Blake Shelton in 2009 called "Hillbilly Bone," which became the first single from Shelton's soon-to-be sixth album. In Extreme Makeover: Home Edition, Adkins made an appearance on October 18, 2009, assisting Ty Pennington and his design team in creating a new house for the Marshall family.

How Trace Adkins Move to Show Dog-Universal Music from 2010 to 2014

Adkins signed with Show Dog-Universal Music in January 2010 after splitting from his longtime record company, Capitol Nashville. "This Ain't No Love Song," Adkins' debut single under the label, was made available on May 17, 2010, and it was the opening track of his ninth studio album, Cowboys Back in Town. In the week of May 29, 2010, it made its chart debut at number 54. On January 10, 2011, "Brown Chicken, Brown Cow," the album's second single, was made available on country radio. Two men were murdered on February 13, 2010, when their Dodge pickup truck collided with a Trace Adkins tour bus. The vehicle is thought to have over a "no overtaking" line in the center of the road, which is why the collision occurred. There were a few Adkins band members on the bus, but none of them had any major injuries. Adkins wasn't on the bus himself when it happened. At the Dallas Cowboys Stadium on October 10, 2010, Adkins performed the national anthem. When Adkins appeared at WWE's yearly spectacular tribute to the Troops on December 18, 2010, the soldiers in attendance gave him an incredible reception. He made a comeback on May 13, 2011, at a Nashville, Tennessee, episode of SmackDown Live, as a special guest of the WWE. Trinity, Adkins' youngest daughter, was featured in the "Just Fishin'" video that was shot on the farm in March 2011. The track peaked at #6 on Billboard. The house of Adkins, located in Brentwood, Tennessee, burnt down on June 4, 2011, at around 3:35 p.m. Adkins sang the national anthem on October 20, 2011, at Game 2 of the 2011 World Series in St. Louis. Adkins dedicated a performance of "One" to Baylor Lady Bears head coach Kim Malkey in April 2011 after acknowledging that he had a crush on her while attending Louisiana Tech University in a Million You " to the former. While everything was going on, Kim Mulkey invited Malkey to perform at Baylor's home game versus Connecticut. Mickey's sister set up a phone call with Kim in December 2011. Adkins made plans to sing the national anthem for the Lady Bears' home game against the Texas A&M Aggies in February 2012 because she was unable to attend. Adkins encouraged the Lady Bears before their NCAA Championship semifinal match in Kansas City in March 2012 while she was visiting the team as part of a tour. Adkins had a cameo vocal appearance on the Meat Loaf album Hell in a Handbasket in February 2012. At a West Virginia Mountaineers home football game versus the Baylor Bears on September 29, 2012, Adkins sang "The Star-Spangled Banner". In the thirty-two-year existence of Mountaineer Field, this was the third live rendition of the national anthem. On May 14, 2013, Adkins's new album, Love Will... May 13, 2013, saw the debut of "Watch the World's End," the album's lead song, on country radio. On the official website, it was stated in September 2013 that he had been taken off the show dog roster. Adkins issued The, his debut Christmas album. October 29, 2013, The King's Gift.

2015 Present: Relocate to Wheelhouse Records

It was revealed on April 6, 2015, that Adkins, going by the moniker Wheelhouse, had signed with Broken Bow Records. Adkins was one of the first musicians to sign to Broken Bow's new label, Wheelhouse Records, the label announced in August 2015. The debut track from the label, "Jesus and Jones," premiered on Country Radio on January 18, 2016, and it reached number 41 on the Country Airplay chart. On July 25, 2016, "Lit" was made available on country radio, however, it failed to chart. The two singles are from the album Something's Going On, which Wheelhouse Records published on March 31, 2017. A music video has been created for the album's title track. Adkins made an unexpected visit to Sarepta, Louisiana's Independence Day celebrations on July 4, 2016. He went on stage with the Backbeat Boogie Band and sang a few songs that weren't prepared. Adkins was featured on Hardy's most recent album, Hicktape Volume

1, in 2019. He and Joe Diffie both appear on the album's track "Redneck Tendencies". Adkins later collaborated with Blake Shelton again in 2019 for the song Hell Light off Shelton's finished album Flurry Loaded: God's Country.

Spokesman

Adkins became the new ambassador for Truckstop Chain Pilot Flying J after agreeing to a contract in 2012. As part of the "Drive a Firestone" campaign to relaunch the brand in 2012, Adkins also provided his distinctive voice to his Firestone.

Television Career

Adkins's television career began when he participated on NBC's "The Celebrity Apprentice" in January 2008. Every famous competitor competed with hopes of raising money for the charity of their choice. Playing in the Food Allergy and Anaphylaxis Network was Adkins. Adkins chose the foundation because his daughter is experiencing potentially fatal allergies to eggs, milk, and peanuts. In the end, he lost to Piers Morgan and came in second place that season. Adkins made a comeback appearance on The All-Star Celebrity Apprentice. As the team's project manager for the first mission, which involved selling meatballs, he set a record for celebrity apprenticeships by generating $670,072 for his charity, the American Red Cross. Adkins advanced to the finals once more (being the first and only finalist in the history of the show) alongside illusionist Penn Jillette from Las Vegas. Adkins prevailed, gaining the title of All-Star Celebrity Apprentice. In addition, he broke the show's record for the most money earned for charity by one individual when he raised $1,524,072 for the American Red Cross. 2019 saw Adkins take on the role of host for INSP's brand-new series, Ultimate Cowboy Showdown. Three seasons of the show were produced.

CHAPTER TWO

Childhood and Early Life

In Sarepta, Webster Parish, north Louisiana, on January 13, 1962, Trace Adkins was born to Aaron Adkins and Peggy Carraway. His dad was employed in a factory.

Adkins was exposed to music from a young age. When he was little, his father taught him the fundamentals of guitar playing. He carried the seed of a musical career inside him thanks to this instruction.

He attended a high school where he participated in the gospel ensemble New Commitments and finished his official schooling. In addition, he was a Future Farmers of America member.
He attended Louisiana Tech University after completing his basic schooling. He was a

defensive end for the university's football team, the Bulldogs.

Trace Adkins Professional Career

He started working on an oil rig even before he finished his degree. Sadly, he injured himself while using a knife to open a pail, losing his little finger in the process. Not to be deterred, he urged the surgeon to fuse the finger so he could carry on with his guitar playing.

In the early 1990s, he performed in honky tonk pubs located in and around Nashville, Tennessee. During these years, he was discovered by a Capitol executive, who signed him to the label.

For this gifted artist, 1996 was a breakout year as he made his debut with the song "There's a Girl in Texas." Soaring to the top of the Billboard Hot Country Singles & Track charts at number 20, the song was an enormous smash.

Later in 1996, he released his debut album, "Dreamin' Out Loud," in response to the enormous popularity of his debut single. The album achieved the same level of success as his first song track, becoming a mega smash and sending several of his singles to the top spot.

Motivated by the commercial success of his first album, he dropped "Big Time," his follow-up. The album was unable to repeat the phenomenal success of his last album, except for one hit, "The Rest of Mine," which peaked at number five.

His third album, "More...", was released in 1999. The album's destiny was similar to that of its predecessor, except for the title tune, and it was not certified gold.

In 2001, he published "Chrome," his fourth album, after an unintentional mistake. The album's title tune was ranked in the Top 10, making it the first to debut in the Top 5 of the country album charts.

In 2003, he released a compilation of his greatest hits album "Comin' on Strong" as a follow-up. The former yielded the song "Then They Do," while the latter produced two singles that peaked at No. 5 and No. 13, respectively, "Hot Mama" and "Rough & Ready."

He provided the voice of KFC for a series of commercials in 2003. He made his television debut in the sitcom "King of the Hill," as Big John. Additionally, he appeared in "Hollywood Squares."

In the TV show "Yes, Dear," he played the role of Curtis, a prisoner, in 2004. In the television series "King of the Hill," he also portrayed Elvin Mackleston.

Regarding his singing career, he put out the album "Songs About Me" in 2005. Its second track, "Honky Tonk Badonkadonk," became a massive crossover smash, while its debut single, "Arlington," sparked controversy. His song debuted in the Top 40 of the Billboard Hot 100 for the first time.

In 2005, he acted in three TV shows: "My Name is Earl," "Blue Collar TV," and "Higglytown Heroes."

His seventh studio album, "Dangerous Man," was released in 2006. On the country charts, "Ladies Love Country Boys" surged to the top, replacing the first single, "Swing," which reached No. 20. His song hit number one for the second time, following the success of the single "No Thinkin' Thing" in 1997.

His 2007 hit, "I Got My Game On," was his creation. Originally intended to be the first single from a new album, "American Man: Greatest Hits, Vol. 2," is the second Greatest Hits compilation featuring the song.

The album's second single, "You're Gonna Miss His," was then made available. Being the fastest-rising single of his, the song peaked at number one on the Hot Country Songs. In addition, it managed to rank in the Top 12 of the Billboard Hot 100 and the Top 19 of the Billboard Pop 100. It reached its peak at number 8 on the Hot Digital Songs chart.

A Personal Stand: Observations and Opinions from a Freethinking Roughneck, his debut book, was published in 2007.

He acted in two major motion pictures in 2008: "Trailer Park of Terror" (as "The Man") and "An American Carol" (as Angel of Death). Additionally, he starred in a single episode of "The Young and the Restless" on television.

He appeared in sixteen episodes of "Celebrity Apprentice" from 2008 to 2011. He participated as a famous competitor in the inaugural season, placing second.

He released the single "Muddy Waters" from the album "X" in 2008. The album featured two Top 20 hits that peaked at No.14: "Marry for Money" together with "All I Ask For Anymore."

He signed a deal with Show Dog-Universal Music in 2010 and left Capitol Nashville. May 2010 saw the release of "This Ain't No Love Song," his debut single from the label. "Cowboy's Back in Town," his second studio album, featured this song as its lead single. On the charts, the album made its debut at number 54.

The Definitive Greatest Hits Til' The Last Shot's Fired, his third compilation album, was released in 2010. He has also performed at Dallas Cowboys Stadium during the National Anthem. Lifted, Tough Trade, and Ace of Cakes are just a few of the movies and TV shows he has acted in. "Proud to Be Here," his tenth studio album, was released in 2011. That same year, he portrayed Eddie Vogel in the motion picture "The Lincoln Lawyer."

2013 saw the release of his first Christmas album, "The King's Gift," as well as two albums, "Love Will." He also produced the compilation album "Icon." In the same year, he played himself in 12 episodes of "All Stars Celebrity Apprentice," where he advanced to the championship round and emerged victorious.

The Walk of Fame in Nashville

Trace Adkins, a multi-platinum-selling country music artist, has found success in his roles as an actor, musician, writer, and performer. He has also earned a spot among the most recognizable and significant country musicians of his generation.

Known for his chart-topping hits, national TV appearances, and wildly successful tours, Adkins is a respected member of the Grand Ole Opry. More than twenty-five of his singles—"Every Light In The House Is On," "(This Ain't) No Thinkin' Thing," "I Left Something Turned On At Home," "Songs About Me," "Honky Tonk Badonkadonk," and "You're Gonna Miss This," which was nominated for three 2008 CMA Awards—have reached the country charts on Billboard.

Thanks to his impressive performance on NBC's popular reality series "The Celebrity Apprentice," Adkins became even more well-known. He went on to win "All-Star Celebrity Apprentice" and donated more than $1.5 million to the American Red Cross and Wounded Warrior Project. Recently, in 2016, Adkins' debut single under Wheelhouse Records, a division of BBR Music Group, was named "Jesus and Jones".

CHAPTER THREE

Track Adkins's Net Worth

American country music singer and actor Trace Adkins has substantial wealth. He has released ten studio albums and two greatest hits compilations during his multi-decade career, enjoying remarkable success in the music business. More than 20 of Adkins' chart-topping singles have kept him atop the Billboard country music charts, establishing him as one of the genre's most important performers.

Trace Adkins's music career has brought him great financial success over the years, as evidenced by his $19 million net worth. "Songs About Me," his best-selling album, is a prime example of his music's commercial success as it has been certified 2× Multi-Platinum. Adkins has also increased his exposure on television, appearing in episodes of hit series like Pyramid and Hollywood Squares.

Showcasing his business savvy and bolstering his already impressive financial portfolio, Trace Adkins won The All-Star Celebrity Apprentice in 2013. Adkins is well-known for his deep bass-baritone voice, which has captured the attention of audiences all over the world, in addition to his professional accomplishments.

At the moment, Brentwood, Tennessee, where Trace Adkins resides, is well known for its wealth. His decision about where to live adds to his overall net worth and signifies his success as an artist. Adkins is a happy husband and father of five children from prior marriages to actress Victoria Pratt.

A testament to his successful career in country music and entertainment is Trace Adkins' $19 million net worth as of 2023. His transition from a little-known singer to a highly esteemed professional is exemplified by his unique musical taste, captivating live performances, and adaptability as an entertainer.

Adkins' influence is not limited to his music; his acting credits and charitable endeavors demonstrate his diverse skill set and dedication to giving back. His resilient and adaptable life story has struck a chord with fans and cemented his standing as a significant player in the country music industry.

Principal Learnings

- At $19 million, American country music singer and actor Trace Adkins is well-off.
- With more than 20 singles that have reached the top of the Billboard country music charts, he has had great success in the music business.
- "Songs About Me," Adkins' best-selling album, is officially certified 2× Multi-Platinum.

- Additionally, he has made appearances on well-known TV programs like Pyramid and Hollywood Squares.
- Within the country music genre, Adkins is unique due to his deep bass-baritone voice.

A Synopsis of Trace Adkins' Musical Career

With his number-one albums and hit singles, Trace Adkins has enjoyed great success in the music industry and has amassed substantial wealth. Adkins has cemented his position in the country music industry with ten studio albums and two greatest hits compilations under his belt. His distinctive deep bass-baritone voice enhances his allure as a performer.

Adkins's "Songs About Me," one of his best-selling albums, has earned a 2× Multi-Platinum certification, demonstrating his adoration among followers. His ability to consistently create music that connects with listeners is demonstrated by the multiple chart-topping singles he has released on the Billboard country music charts.

Adkins's success in the music business has improved his financial situation in addition to giving him notoriety. He has amassed an impressive $19 million in net worth through his concert tours, album sales, and other music-related endeavors. Adkins will likely keep increasing his net worth in the years to come given his continued involvement in the country music industry.

Certification of the Album

- Songs About Me 2× Multi-Platinum
- Strong Note with Platinum
- Dangerous Man Platinum
- Chrome Gold

Adkins has achieved success outside of the music business by making appearances on TV programs like Pyramid and Hollywood Squares. He demonstrated his talent and versatility even more in 2013 when he won The All-Star Celebrity Apprentice.

Baritone Voice with Deep Bass

A key component of Adkins' allure and the reason for his success in the country music industry is his rich bass-baritone voice. His unique vocal style makes him stand out from other musicians and has won him a devoted following.

Top-Charting Records and Accolades

Trace Adkins has amassed an impressive net worth over his career with the release of several chart-topping albums. Adkins has established himself as a major player in the country music industry with the release of ten studio albums and two greatest hits compilations. His albums have risen to the top of the Billboard charts thanks to the popularity of his relatable lyrics and deep bass-baritone voice.

"Songs About Me," one of Adkins' best-selling albums, has received a 2× Multi-Platinum certification. This record demonstrated Adkins's storytelling prowess and achieved considerable commercial success. Adkins' status in the country music industry was cemented when his hit song "Songs About Me" shot to the top thanks to his potent voice, intriguing songwriting, and devoted fan following.

Trace Adkins has won multiple awards for his music throughout his career. He has received recognition from organizations like the Country Music Association (CMA) and the Academy of Country Music (ACM). Adkins's certifications and chart-topping albums show off his talent and add a substantial amount to his total net worth.

Discography of the Album

- Speaking My Dreams AloudGold
- Very, very big gold.
- Chrome Gold Comes Back With Powerful Gold Songs About Me 2× Multi-Platinum
- Risky IndividualX Gold
- I'm Glad to Be Here, Gold Love Will. Gold.
- There's a Gold Thing Afoot

The certifications and chart-topping albums of Trace Adkins attest to his continued success in the music business. He has become one of the most respected musicians in country music thanks to his ability to connect with listeners through his strong vocals and relatable songs.

How Much does Trace Adkins Make

Trace Adkins's career in music and entertainment is the main source of his income. His income is derived from concert appearances, album sales, and royalties from his vast discography. Adkins's strict touring schedule is well-known, and it makes a substantial financial contribution. In addition, he makes money from his work in movies and television, including acting parts and cameos on programs like "The Celebrity Apprentice."

Adkins also receives compensation from endorsements and merchandise sales. His varied career in entertainment and music has been financially fulfilling even though precise numbers regarding his earnings per project are not made public.

Nomination for a Grammy

Trace Adkins's manager at the time, Gary Borman, pulled him aside early in the player's career and offered some wise counsel.

Adkins spoke with The Park Record over the phone from his tour bus in Oregon, saying, "I remember one day he pointed toward the television and said, 'Be on that little box as much as you can." "I haven't forgotten that, and I've seized the majority of the opportunities that have presented themselves."

Adkins isn't just a country singer nominated for a Grammy Award because of this. In addition to acting, the former oil rigger has starred in films like "The Lincoln Lawyer."

Matthew McConaughey and "Mom's Night Out," starring Sarah Drew, Patricia Heaton, and Sean Astin.
Adkins appeared on a season of "Celebrity Apprentice," and his rich southern drawl can also be heard in Firestone tire advertising.

He declared, "I vowed not to do that again because there have been some that have been too far out." Though it would have to include a philanthropic component, I'm not saying I would never do another reality program. It would need to possess some sort of redeeming characteristic. That hasn't materialized thus far.

Adkins' greatest hits event, which will feature songs like "You're Gonna Miss This," "Ladies Love Country Boys," and maybe the newest single, "Lit," will take place at Deer Valley's Snow Park Amphitheater on Thursday, August 25. This will be Park City's next opportunity to see him live.

About the next show, he stated, "We know what the fans want to hear." As a lover of country music, I want to hear the hits when I see a performer I've been admiring for twenty years. We won't overwhelm them with too many new items, but we might add a few new ones.

Nevertheless, Adkins recognizes similarities between his live music performances and his cinematic acting roles when he steps onto the stage.

"Regardless of the topic of the tune, you need to attempt to genuinely place yourself in that place while you're not kidding," he said. "I always thought that the audience could tell if you were trying too hard.

Acting is the same way, according to Adkins. "You have to become the character and fully engage with the dialogue.

He laughed and remarked, "The instant gratification you get from applause is the part where it doesn't weave together so well." That's not something you see in a TV show or film. You'll undoubtedly hear comments like "Well, that was pretty good" or "Do that again."

Adkins needs to be aware. He has given performances throughout the world, including yearly USO tours that have taken him to the Middle East, where he was just a month ago.

"We've been doing those for around 15 years now," he said. We frequently do big international tours in the United States, averaging one each year.

He has never performed like that before, save for those gigs.

"You will want to go back and do it again once you do one of those things and you get to play for the most appreciative audience you have ever played for," Adkins remarked.
The performer is continuously affected by such tours even after they end.

Adkins recalled having the chance to talk with Wayne Newton—who sort of replaced Bob Hope as the USO guy—before embarking on his first mission to find out what to anticipate. "You should expect to feel bad when you get home," he warned.
"What's he talking about?" I asked myself.
Adkins had no trouble understanding Newton's meaning when the trip was over.

Adkins communicated, "It seems like they [the swarm members] give more to you, paying little regard to the sum you give of yourself or how hard you play." " Not only had everything taken place when I returned home, but neither they nor I were home.

According to Adkins, performers must raise the spirits of soldiers defending the country.

"I accept it is our obligation as a group to give those serving access the tactical knowledge that we are considering them and that we have people in danger," he stated. "Every opportunity we have, we have to give them a small taste of home and assist them in putting their important work on hold for a little while to decompress and unwind. There's also a chance to thank those on stage.

The National Defense Industrial Association honored Adkins with the Dwight D. Eisenhower Award earlier this year in recognition of his commitment to, support of, and advocacy for the country's military personnel.

Being the third performer to win the prize, he expressed his embarrassment by saying he was "really embarrassed."

In terms of performers, Adkins stated that Bob Hope was the first and Gary Sinise the second. Then, by mistake, it was given to me.

He remarked, "It's overwhelming to be on the list with former presidents, chiefs of staff, and four-star generals." Although I went and respectfully received it, it's difficult to compartmentalize it. I genuinely appreciate it so much.

Adkins is looking forward to a new album's release in the interim.

"I've finished my parts and submitted it," he declared. "I finished it, but I don't know when it will be released."

According to Adkins, creating albums is the most satisfying part of the work.

He laughed and remarked, "That's the one thing that hasn't changed over the years, aside from the fact that I'm not as nervous." My favorite thing to do in the music industry is still going into the studio on tracking days, getting down on tracks with ten or twelve of the greatest musicians on the planet.

That is his favorite day, he declared. "It's the most stimulating [experience] you will ever have because of the level of creativity and talent in that room."
These sessions are similar to Adkins' career-long practice of performing alongside his idols.

"Having fun and collaborating with one of your peers is always enjoyable," he remarked. "Performances with my idols, Merle Haggard, Buck Owens, Ed Bruce, and George Jones, are among my most treasured and esteemed recollections as a fan of country music.

"I would have been happy if my career had ended after just one of those because I got to go on stage and sing with those guys," he remarked. But for now, Adkins is focused on the Beehive State.
"We're excited to return to Utah," he remarked. We adore that location.

CHAPTER FOUR

The History of Trace Adkins Family

Trace's wife. Actress Victoria, 51, has several credits in the film industry, such as Day Break, Heartland, and Mutant X. According to rumors, the two met while filming the 2014 film The Virginian.

For Trace, Victoria is his "muse." "I can't even begin to explain what a difference she's made in my life," he stated in a People interview. Her presence revitalized me and motivated me to maximize the remaining time I had, then just create the greatest music I can."

Trace and Victoria married in New Orleans in October 2019. Blake Shelton, a friend of Trace and another country music artist, presided over the wedding. Trace stated that he wouldn't object to Blake appearing as a guest star on Monarch. Distractify claims that he stated, "I believe Blake Shelton should be brought in and given the role of my foolish younger brother. Well, that's kind of who he is."

Was Trace Adkins previously married?

Indeed, this is Trace's fourth union. In 1982, he wed Barbara Lewis, his high school love, before this. Following their eventual divorce, he wed Julie Curtis from 1991 until 1994. Later, from 1997 until 2015, he wed Rhonda Forlaw. Victoria is getting married again. She was formerly wed from 2000 until 2016 by filmmaker and photographer T. J. Scott.

Trace Adkins Children's

The 60-year-old is the mother of five girls! Together, he and Barbara have two daughters:

Tarah and Sarah. Trace is now a grandfather because Tarah and Sarah both have their children. Mackenzie, Brianna, and Trinity were his other three daughters from his marriage to Rhonda.

Trace Adkins, the country music star, is a happy father! He is a loving parent in between his jaw-dropping shows, even if his five kids are now adults. With his first wife, Barbara Lewis, Trace had two daughters: Tarah and Sarah. With his third wife, Rhonda Forlaw, he gained three daughters: Mackenzie, Briana, and Trinity.

Actress Victoria Pratt, Trace's fourth wife, and he are now happily married. Trace is a happy father who is witnessing his girls grow up in front of him. Trace, meanwhile, will be the first to admit that his early struggles with alcoholism caused him to resign from parenting following the birth of his first two kids.

They are aware of it and take full advantage of it, which makes me feel awful about it. In a 2007 interview with Country Weekly, he said, "I tell them 'no' very seldom." But the fact that my three younger daughters have a father and my elder two does not make me feel bad. Not only is drinking and other related behaviors important, but age is another factor. I was a young man. I had not yet established my identity. I was still searching for my identity and purpose in life, still stumbling and feeling my way through the dark.

Over 11 million records have been sold by the multi-platinum recording artist since his 1996 country music debut. Trace has won several accolades and produced chart-topping tunes in collaboration with artists such as Blake Shelton, Luke Bryan, and Snoop Dogg. With his children's and grandkids' help, he intends to carry on his legacy for many more years.

In an August 2021 interview with Music Row, Trace stated, "I'm looking forward to being 80 years old and walking out on the stage of the Grand Ole Opry." "I am going to dance to Honky

Tonk Badonkadonk outside and cause embarrassment to my grandchildren."

Every time Trace takes the stage, he embraces his upbeat character and raspy voice, which have made him well-known. In a 2017 interview with Taste of Country, he did, however, acknowledge that he is attempting to instill one very funny lesson in all of his grandchildren: "To be quiet." No one else is attempting to educate them to be silent, so that is what I try to do.

Webber, Tarah Adkins

Born in 1983, Tarah Adkins Webber is the oldest of Trace and Julie's daughters. David Webber, Tarah's spouse, is the parent of three children. She has a good bond with her younger sister Sarah. The couple were married on July 1, 2007. Tarah supports her dad in all he does by posting pictures and videos of him on Facebook.

Taste of Country questioned if he pampered his grandchildren.

He assured the interviewer, "Not too much, not too much." "I suppose they get anything they want, but I don't go crazy. There isn't much left to do because they are spoiled anyhow. Their parents have already given them an excessive amount of spoiling. Thus, they don't require my assistance.

Sarah Beth Adkins

Born in 1985, Sarah Beth Adkins is Trace and Julie's youngest daughter. Sarah frequently posts pictures of her family on Facebook since she is a proud mother. She disclosed in a September 2021 post that she had recorded backing vocals for Trace's song "So Do The Neighbors." She made a backstage photo visit at Trace and Blake's concert the same month. She related a tale of her father forgetting her birthday.

I said to Blake that I would have appreciated it if he had wished me a happy birthday tonight. "Yes, Monday is her birthday," his father said when he asked Trace whether she knew it was her daughter's birthday. But I have no idea how old she will be," Sarah said, causing Blake to chuckle. "I'm only one out of five. These days, Dad, it's simply a number.

The Mackenzie Lynn Adkins

Born in 1998, Lynn Adkins is the eldest child of Trace and Rhonda. As of right now, Mackenzie resides in Nashville, TN. To commemorate Mackenzie's University of Tennessee graduation, Trace posted an uncommon Instagram picture of her in October 2020.

"Congratulations to @mackenzielynnadkins, my lovely daughter! Her degree from the University of Tennessee was just received. I'm pleased with you! in the post's caption.

When a home fire broke out in the garage in 2011, Mackenzie and her younger sisters managed to escape. Together with their canines, the girls made a safe exit using the techniques they had learned at school.

Briana Rhea Adkins

Born in 2001, Briana Rhea Adkins is the second youngest daughter of Trace and Rhonda. In 2009, she appeared in Trace's "Ladies Love Country Boys" music video. Following her sisters' survival in the home fire, Briana received the PETA Compassionate Action Award in recognition of her assistance in rescuing the family's animals.

Briana is currently a model with Nashville's AMAX. She shared stunning pictures of herself modeling on Instagram. In 2019, Briana received a unique direct message from her father on Twitter. Trace expressed his pride in her for her significant achievement in a letter.

Lee Adkins, Trinity

Born in 2004, Trace and Rhonda's youngest child is Trinity Lee Adkins. 2011 saw her in his music video for "Just Fishin." Trace has taken cues from his daughters when it comes to making songs throughout his career. His song "Then They Do" is about witnessing his kids grow up and eventually get married.

Celebrity Apprentice Win and Appearances

Through his appearances on well-known television programs and his victory on The All-Star Celebrity Apprentice, Trace Adkins has demonstrated his talent outside of the music business. Because of his charm and singing ability, he is a sought-after guest on shows like Hollywood Squares and Pyramid, where his captivating presence enthralls audiences.

Adkins's successful tenure on The All-Star Celebrity Apprentice in 2013 served as more evidence of his versatility as an artist. Business tycoon Donald Trump served as the show's presenter, matching up famous competitors in a series of tasks designed to generate money for the charity of their choice. Adkins triumphed, winning over Trump and the audience with his cunning plan and unflinching resolve.

In addition to increasing Adkins' wealth and financial standing, his popularity on television has grown. He has further cemented his status as a cherished figure in the entertainment world by exhibiting his adaptability and endearing demeanor.

Voice and Musical Style: Deep Bass-Baritone
A characteristic that sets Trace Adkins apart is his rich, bass-baritone voice, which has won him a devoted following and helped him succeed financially. In the country music scene, Adkins stands out thanks to his distinctive singing style, which connects with listeners and leaves a lasting impression. He has become a well-known

name in the industry because of his ability to attract people with his strong voice.

Adkins' sound is unique and appealing to a broad audience since it combines parts of conventional country music with elements of rock and gospel. His deep, resonant voice gives his compositions a feeling of realism and intimacy by adding depth and passion. Adkins has achieved both economic success and critical recognition for his ability to portray sincere words through his strong vocals.

Adkins has established himself as one of the biggest acts in country music with several chart-topping singles and albums during his career. His CD "Songs About Me" became certified 2× Multi-Platinum and was quite successful. The sales of his songs, his tour dates, and his royalties have all had a significant impact on Adkins' net worth.

Songs About Me 2× Multi-Platinum Album Certification: Vibrant Gold Dangerous Man

Trace Adkins has achieved financial success because of his musical talents, unique voice, and genre-bending approach. His devoted following keeps him going, which enables him to continue being a major player in the country music scene.

Trace Adkins has demonstrated the financial obligations that accompany his personal life by being married numerous times and having five children. Tarah and Sarah, his two kids from his previous marriage, were born to Barbara Lewis. He wed Julie Curtis a second time, and the two of them had three daughters: MacKenzie, Brianna, and Trinity. Adkins needs to arrange his finances and provide for his children because of his blended family and marriages.

Adkins has five children, so he has to think about their general upbringing, medical requirements, and educational needs. There may be child support duties associated with every marriage, which may include costs for housing, schooling, health insurance, and extracurricular activities. The significance of Adkins' prosperous music career and his capacity to support his family are further highlighted by these financial obligations.

Adkins has maintained a prosperous career in the music business despite his financial responsibilities, which enables him to sustain his family and have a nice life. His multiple albums and chart-topping singles have greatly increased his net worth, allowing him to satisfy the financial obligations resulting from his personal life.

Residence in Brentwood, Tennessee

Living in Brentwood, Tennessee, an affluent community, enhances Trace Adkins's reputation as a prosperous and well-mannered person. Brentwood, a wealthy neighborhood, is well-known for drawing well-known people from a range of fields, including business, sports, and entertainment. For anyone looking for seclusion and a high level of life, the city's stunning scenery, opulent estates, and proximity to Nashville make it the perfect destination.

Trace Adkins has a luxurious and opulent lifestyle in Brentwood, which is a reflection of his success in the music business. The city's standing complements his career as a well-known actor and singer of country music, which boosts his public image and adds to his total net worth.

An insight into Trace Adkins's personal life and the associated financial obligations may be gained from his Brentwood, Tennessee, home. Property taxes, upkeep expenditures, and other related fees are probably high for owners of real estate in such a posh neighborhood. But it also shows that he can maintain and finance such an opulent lifestyle, underscoring his ongoing success and sound financial standing.

Brentwood, Tennessee Home of Trace Adkins Features Location Estimated Value

Brentwood, Tenn. a posh neighborhood
renowned for its exquisite homes and lovely
surroundings five million dollars

CHAPTER FIVE

A Successful Music Career S Effect on Net Worth

Trace Adkins' remarkable net worth has been mostly contributed to by his successful music career. Adkins is an American actor and singer of country music who has been in several major films and has over 20 number-one hits on the Billboard country music charts. A major factor in his financial success has been his best-selling album, "Songs About Me," which has been certified 2× Multi-Platinum.

Adkins has amassed significant wealth through his singing career in addition to priceless possessions. His financial situation demonstrates a financially fulfilling career and is a tribute to his skill and diligence in the field. Adkins' success as a country music performer has had a significant effect on his wealth and income.

Beyond his musical career, Trace Adkins has amassed a fortune through a variety of endeavors, including TV appearances and his 2013 victory on The All-Star Celebrity Apprentice. These other revenue streams have increased his net worth and cemented his place in the entertainment industry.

Principal Aspects Affecting Trace Adkins' Net Worth Specifics

Music ProfessionalismAdkins' substantial net worth has been bolstered by his successful albums, chart-topping songs, and certifications.

On-TV PresencesAdkins now has more revenue streams and a better financial situation overall because of his appearances on well-liked television programs.

Company AttemptsAdkins's financial wealth has grown as a result of his participation in endorsement deals and entrepreneurial endeavors.

Adkins has demonstrated his capacity to give back to society by supporting several philanthropic initiatives as a philanthropist.

Trace Adkins's music career continues to have a significant influence on his net worth due to his remarkable wealth and continued success. He will undoubtedly continue to amass wealth and establish himself as a major player in the country music industry as he takes on new endeavors and develops his abilities.

List of Accomplishments
- 20 chart-topping songs on the Billboard country music charts, respectively.
- 2013's All-Star Celebrity Apprentice winner,
- Certified 2× Multi-Platinum for his album "Songs About Me"

Philanthropic Activities and Donations

Notwithstanding his fortune, Trace Adkins is renowned for his charitable endeavors and constructive contributions to society. He thinks it's important to help those in need by leveraging his platform and accomplishments. Throughout his career, Adkins has been active in several philanthropic organizations and events, utilizing his platform to help issues near and dear to his heart get more attention and funding.

Trace Adkins is an ardent supporter of several charities, including the American Red Cross. He has been actively involved in fundraising initiatives to offer help and support to individuals impacted by natural disasters, such as hurricanes, floods, and wildfires, as a strong champion for disaster relief operations. Adkins is aware of the value of aiding communities in their efforts to rebuild and recover after adversity.

Furthermore, Trace Adkins is a supporter of the Wounded Warrior Project, a group that helps injured warriors by offering guidance and services. Adkins has contributed to the cause of veterans' rights and welfare by playing at some benefit concerts and events. He thinks it is important to remember and encourage those who have defended their nation.

Contribution of Organization

- The Red Cross in America participates in campaigns to raise money for disaster relief initiatives
- Wounded Warrior Project Attendance at benefit performances and other gatherings for injured soldiers
- Other Organizations That Promote Charity Contributions and backing many humanitarian endeavors

Trace Adkins is devoted to improving the lives of others, as seen by his charitable activities. He continues to encourage people to offer assistance and effect significant change through his kind donations and encouragement. Trace Adkins has achieved financial success, but he doesn't lose focus on his commitment to utilize his power for the greater good.

Prospective Projects and Their Possible Effect on Net Worth

Trace Adkins's net worth can rise in the future with more unfinished business and achievements. Adkins has made a name for himself in the country music business because of his critically acclaimed albums and rich bass-baritone voice. His successes in music have had a significant impact on his financial situation, demonstrating the value of his money.

Adkins's continued professional pursuits portend more wealth accumulation. His stirring lyrics and strong voice never fail to enthrall audiences, and he has amassed a devoted following throughout the globe. His fortune and assets should rise as he takes on new endeavors and puts out more songs.

Adkins is a well-known television personality in addition to his singing career. He even won The All-Star Celebrity Apprentice in 2013. His total financial success has been aided by these pursuits, which have produced extra revenue streams.

Living in Brentwood, Tennessee, a wealthy suburb, Adkins has placed himself in a neighborhood that is recognized for its riches. Putting himself in the company of like-minded people who place a high value on achievement and financial prosperity may have further improved his financial situation.

Assets, Net Worth, and EarningsIncome and Financial StatusFortune

Wealthy Net Worth of $19 million career in music and on television appearancesReal estate and financial investments

Due to Trace Adkins' skill, achievements, and astute decisions, his net worth is expected to increase. His estimated net worth is projected to rise as he pursues new ventures and builds on his achievements, securing his standing as one of the most renowned musicians in country music.

Challenges in Personal and Health

Adkins has struggled with alcoholism and other personal problems, such as health problems. Fans have responded well to his candor about these difficulties, which has enhanced his public presence.

Activism and Philanthropy

Adkins is renowned for his charitable endeavors as well, especially those that benefit military families and veterans. His dedication to giving back and championing causes near and dear is evident in his advocacy efforts.

Key Points

- *Hit Singles:* Distinguished by top-charting songs such as "Honky Tonk Badonkadonk."
- *Dynamic performer:* Known for his fascinating live performances, this is well-known.
- *Acting Career:* Successfully entered the television and movie industries.
- *Philanthropic Efforts:* Engaged in active support of several charitable organizations.
- *Wide Range of Music:* Several CDs with a fusion of modern and traditional country music were released.
- *Overcoming Obstacles:* Along the way, he has had to overcome both personal and medical obstacles.

- *Deep connection with his fan base*: he is well-known for this.
- *Television Appearances:* Made more appearances on reality TV and attracted more attention.
- *Easily Recognizable Voice:* His rich, baritone voice is well-known.
- *Longevity in Music:* Continued to be a steady force in the country music scene.

CHAPTER SIX

Trace Adkins' 24-year career is being showcased at Kansas Crossing Casino.

PITTSBURG, Kansas: He has voiced characters for animated series like "King of the Hill" and "American Dad!" He acted in films such as "The Lincoln Lawyer" and small-screen comedies such as "My Name Is Earl." On "Celebrity Apprentice," he sat across from Donald Trump in the boardroom.

Without a doubt, though, 60-year-old Trace Adkins is at his finest when performing humorous or genuinely depressing country songs live. He'll be playing both on Saturday starting at 7:30 p.m. at Kansas Crossing Casino's Outdoor Corral stage.

Adkins is spending one night on his "The Way I Wanna Go" tour in Southeast Kansas. As the tour's name suggests, he's in a position in his work to pursue his interests and is enjoying himself immensely.

According to the multi-platinum award winner, "I've got to the point where it's all up to me now." "I am free to do what I like... and it's a lovely place to be.

Adkins first gained popularity in the mid-1990s during the height of country music. His "Dreamin' Out Loud" album, released in 1996, had four number-one hits, including "Every Light in the House" and "(This Ain't) No Thinkin' Thing." Adkins distinguished himself from the other male country musicians of the day not just with these songs but also with his powerful baritone and 6-foot-6-inch stature. The singer-performer's mystique was further enhanced by his black cowboy hat, which gave him an extra 2 inches of height.

The 2021 album "The Way I Wanna Go," Adkins' 17th studio album with 25 songs, including "Heartbreak Song" and "Where I am Today," will be mixed with some of his well-known early tunes at Kansas Crossing include "I Left Something Turned On at Home," "Help Me Understand," "There's a Girl in Texas," "Honky Tonk Badonkadonk," and "Lonely Won't Leave Me Alone."

Adkins declared, "I am currently at the top of my game." "This is the best I've ever been at anything, and I think my voice sounds better now than it did 25 years ago."
Over nearly 24 years, Adkins has sold over 11 million albums and charted more than 37 singles, 14 of which have made it into Billboard's Top 10.

"I love where I am right now," Adkins said. "Despite having the perfect job, I'm not sure where I'll fit in when the history of my work is written. However, ninety percent of the time, I stated what I wanted to say, stood by my convictions, and accomplished my goals. I will also end my life in the manner that I want.

Country Music Is Still Awesome

After ten years of becoming a country music chart-topper, racking up several hit songs and nine platinum albums, Trace Adkins is determined not to let anything pass him by.

"We like to stay busy all the time -- I'm aware that a career in this business is a finite thing," remarked Adkins.

Adkins has decades more of singing ahead of her, according to those who love country music.

It's a common misconception in the show industry that Adkins' 1996 breakthrough and hit song, "(This Ain't) No Thinkin' Thing," sent him skyrocketing to the top of the charts; in reality, he had been performing for ten years. A decade spent touring the honky tonk circuit—just another sudden success story?

The native of Springhill, Louisiana, Adkins recalled, "I worked a lot of Jamborees and such as a young man. I played bass in a gospel quartet originally." "I started playing in clubs around 1986, around Texas and Louisiana -- I've been doing this a long time."

Adkins didn't know he would become a professional musician right away, despite coming from a musical background. Following his graduation from Louisiana Tech University, he worked for several years as a pipefitter on offshore oil drilling rigs, where he studied petroleum technology. Adkins had been bitten by the music bug enough by 1992 to relocate to Nashville, but he still needed to work during the day as a builder to make ends meet.

Scott Hendricks, the president of Capitol Records at the time, saw Adkins perform at a juke joint outside of Nashville in 1995 and was immediately struck by his powerful voice and working-class mentality. This was Adkins's big break. His first album, "Dreamin' Out Loud," was making progress on the charts in less than a year. Four of Adkins' debut album's hits made it into the top 20 country charts.

Given that several of his greatest singles would have been classified as country rock thirty years ago, Adkins, forty-five, is a shining illustration of how rock 'n' roll has changed the nation.

"I think that's just because a lot of people who grew up in the 1970s and '80s, listening to a lot of good rock 'n' roll, have all ended up here in country music now," Adkins explained. "I agree that many of us were referred to as rock bands in the past. Half a century ago, Rascal Flatts would have been classified as a rock group. The primary reason, in my opinion, is that Nashville now has producers who are at the top of their game and who all come from the same generation that was raised in that genre of music. The sound that comes through in their work is that of the classic rock era of the 1970s and 1980s, which has greatly affected them all and helped them to refine their art."

Adkins said that even if CD sales are declining due to alternative music distribution channels and the broader downturn in the music industry, country music is still prospering.

"I don't honestly think country music has ever been any healthier than it is right now," he added.

"Country-western music is popular in America, and according to Pollstar, these genres' tours have the highest attendance rates. That's probably because country music appeals to a wider audience than any other genre. While other genres have a more exclusive appeal, country music is currently so broad that a wide range of styles may fit inside it. Country music encompasses a wide range of styles."

A recent development in Adkins' career is the emergence of ringtones as a side project for successful tracks. "Honky Tonk Badonkadonk" was downloaded as a ringtone by over 75,000 individuals in just six weeks after its debut. Pop and hip-hop often dominate the national ringtone charts, where the song peaked at number 15. This appeal contributed to the ongoing sales of his most recent CD, "Dangerous Man," which came out last year and has since produced three smash songs.

"There's no way I could have ever seen that ringtone thing coming," Adkins replied. "That's a whole new wrinkle that's been extended into the game."

Adkins is one of those famous people in Nashville who gets his fresh content from a consistent group of composers. Intriguing songs he's recorded throughout the years include "Arlington," a 2005 song spoken from the perspective of a soldier getting ready to be buried in Arlington National Cemetery. His most recent album's lead tune, "Swing," draws parallels between love relationships and baseball. "I Wanna Feel Something," his latest hit, articulates a need for genuine feeling in our fast-paced, manufactured contemporary society.

"We've found a few writers in town that write in that vein, that can produce songs that are right in my wheelhouse as a singer," Adkins added.

Adkins stated that he is almost halfway through the process of recording his second album, and he has scheduled studio time for this summer to complete the process.

A Christmas gospel album is something Adkins would want to make eventually. "I think we've recorded a couple of future hits already," he added.

Trace Adkins, however, is still loving the trip and being a voice for the average person more than ten years into his music career.

"I'm pretty proud that I fulfilled my original, 1996 seven-album deal," stated the musician. "That is a true accomplishment in our industry because not many people get to do that." I'm aware of how fortunate I am to be making a livelihood doing this since I immediately re-upped for another five-album agreement. And I do think of myself as a blue-collar man singing about topics that other blue-collar folks can relate to."

CONCLUSION

Trace Adkins's financial success as a country singer has been cemented by his accomplishments in the music business, television appearances, and personal connections, all of which have contributed to his considerable net worth. Adkins has made a name for himself in the country music industry and is worth a reported $19 million. His total income has increased as a result of his 10 studio albums, two greatest hits collections, and many number-one songs.

Adkins has earned extra money with his television performances on shows like Pyramid and Hollywood Squares in addition to his singing career. In addition to showcasing his abilities outside of music, his victory on The All-Star Celebrity Apprentice in 2013 increased his already substantial wealth.

Adkins' distinctive musical style, which has found a home with admirers all over the world and contributed to his financial success, is well-known for his deep bass-baritone voice. His unique vocal style and appealing stage presence have helped him become more well-known and have raised his earning potential.

Adkins's personal life and family relationships also affect his financial situation, even if his career accomplishments have surely had a major impact. Adkins has financial duties and commitments that highlight the significance of his riches, including five children from prior marriages and a current marriage to actress Victoria Pratt.

Adkins, who lives in Brentwood, Tennessee, one of the wealthiest communities in the country, has made this decision. This geographical decision demonstrates his desire for a luxurious lifestyle and also indicates how valuable he is financially.

Adkins shows his dedication to giving back to the community via his charitable activities and efforts. His ability to help others in need is made possible by his financial prosperity.

Projects in the works by Adkins might see more financial expansion in the future. His net worth is projected to rise as he pursues new endeavors and grows his career, securing his standing as a prosperous country music artist.

Happy Reading! ♥

Made in United States
Troutdale, OR
11/15/2024